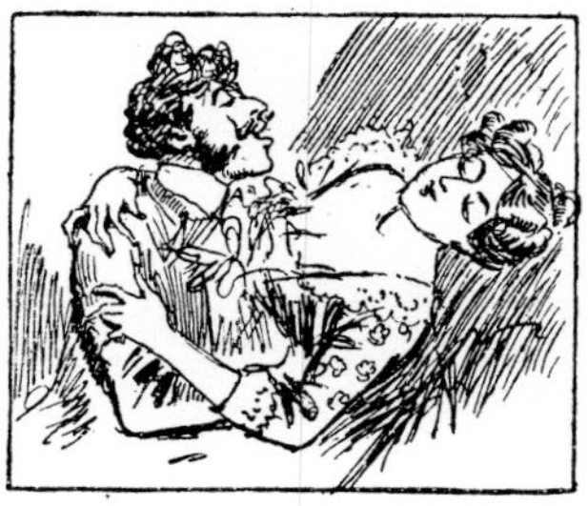

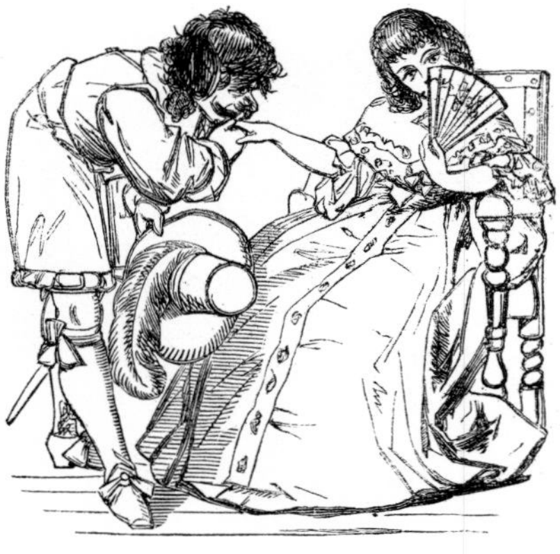

HYP

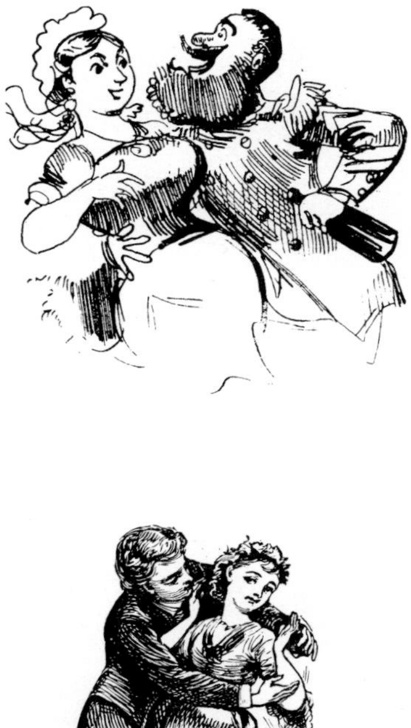

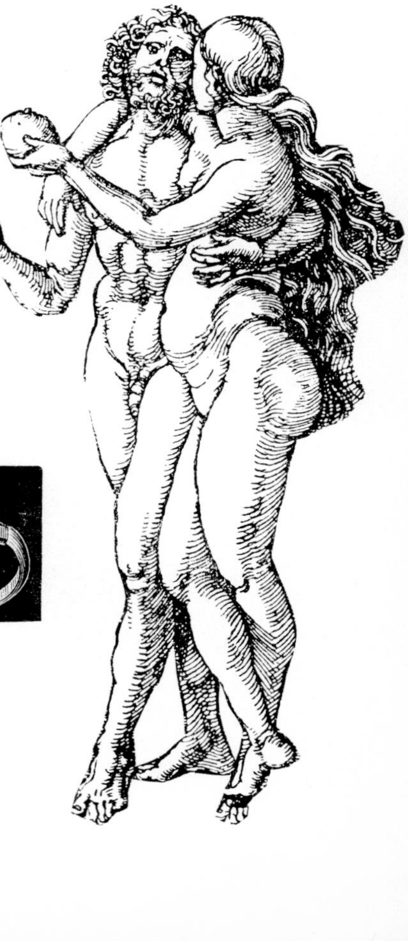

-HYP-

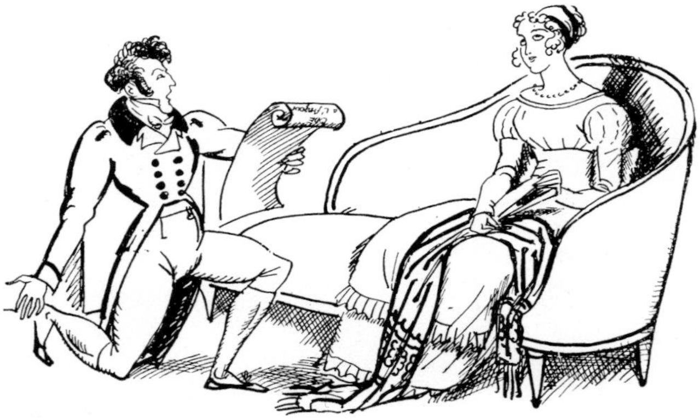

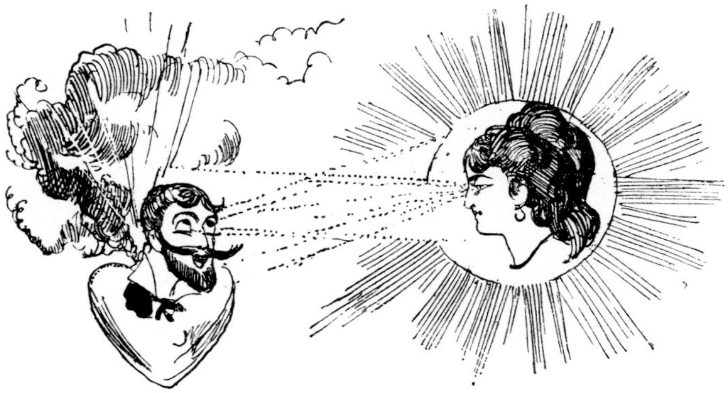

TOOTSIE'S
LETTER - BOX

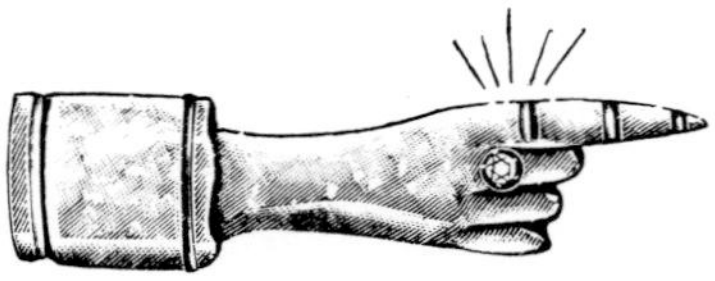

SAINT
VALENTINE

VIOLET
TOILET WATER
COLGATE & Co
NEW YORK

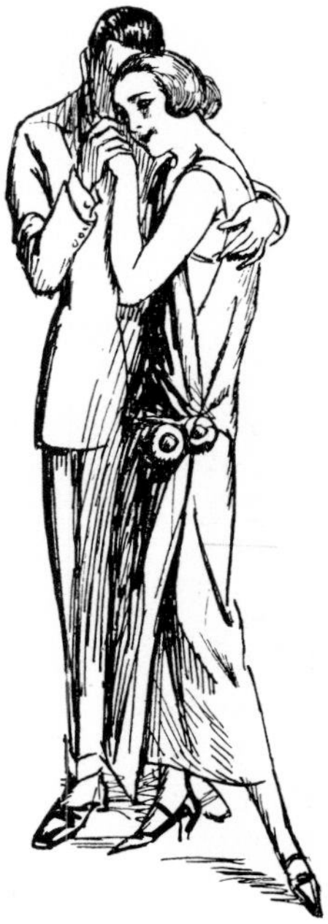

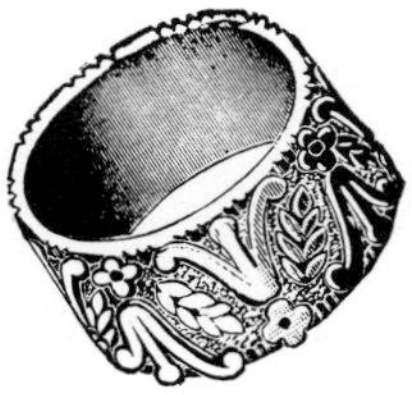